Scripture S

Primary
Volume V

Psalms & Proverbs

for

Young Catholics

CONCEIVED & WRITTEN BY
MARY ELLEN TEDROW-WYNN

COVER, LAYOUT DESIGN, & TYPESETTING BY
ALLISON ARMERDING

Dedication

To all my Catholic family and friends:
May God bless you as you search for the truth in HIM.

John 14:6 (In speaking to Thomas):
Jesus saith to him: I am the way, and the truth, and the life.
No man cometh to the Father, but by me.

Copyright

Scripture Scribes: Psalms & Proverbs for Young Catholics
Laurelwood Books © 2016
ISBN: 978-1-941383-35-3

We have checked for errors in this text.
However, should you notice any mistakes, we would love to hear from you.
Please contact us at *marylnw7@gmail.com*.

All Scripture taken from the Douay Rheims 1899 American Version.
Public Domain.

Not to be reproduced without express written permission from the publisher.
Thank you for respecting this.
Schools and/or co-ops, please contact us for group discounts.

Find this and other great books on our website:
www.laurelwoodbooks.com
You may also reach us at:
Laurelwood Books
1639 Ebenezer Road
Bluemont, VA 20135

Scripture Scribes

Scripture Scribes is copy work for students to write and fall in love with the Scriptures.

Scripture Scribes: Psalms & Proverbs for Young Catholics features:

- 30 lessons using the Douay Rheims Version of the Bible
- Reading Scripture
- Tracing Scripture
- Copying Scripture

Lesson 1: Day 1

> Therefore the wicked shall not rise again in judgment:
> nor sinners in the council of the just.
> Psalm 1:5

Trace and copy the verse below.

Psalms & Proverbs for Young Catholics © 2016 Not to be reproduced.

Lesson 1: Day 2

> For the Lord knoweth the way of the just:
> and the way of the wicked shall perish.
> Psalm 1:6

Trace and copy the verse below.

For the Lord knoweth the way

of the just: and the way of

the wicked shall perish.

For the Lord knoweth the way

of the just: and the way of

the wicked shall perish.

Lesson 1: Day 3

> And now, O ye kings, understand:
> receive instruction, you that judge the earth.
> Psalm 2:10

Trace and copy the verse below.

Lesson 1: Day 4

> Serve ye the Lord with fear:
> and rejoice unto him with trembling.
> Psalm 2:11

Trace and copy the verse below.

Serve ye the Lord with fear:

and rejoice unto him

with trembling.

Serve ye the Lord with fear:

and rejoice unto him

with trembling.

Lesson 2: Day 1

> The fear of the Lord is the beginning of wisdom.
> Fools despise wisdom and instruction.
> Proverbs 1:7

Trace and copy the verse below.

The fear of the Lord is the

beginning of wisdom. Fools

despise wisdom and instruction.

The fear of the Lord is the

beginning of wisdom. Fools

despise wisdom and instruction.

Lesson 2: Day 2

> My son, hear the instruction of thy father,
> and forsake not the law of thy mother:
> Proverbs 1:8

Trace and copy the verse below.

My son, hear the instruction of

thy father, and forsake not

the law of thy mother:

instruction: teaching

My son, hear the instruction of

thy father, and forsake not

the law of thy mother:

Lesson 2: Day 3

> My son, forget not my law,
> and let thy heart keep my commandments.
> Proverbs 3:1

Trace and copy the verse below.

My son, forget not my law,

and let thy heart

keep my commandments.

My son, forget not my law,

and let thy heart

keep my commandments.

Lesson 2: Day 4

> For they shall add to thee length of days,
> and years of life and peace.
> Proverbs 3:2

Trace and copy the verse below.

For they shall add to thee

length of days, and years

of life and peace.

For they shall add to thee

length of days, and years

of life and peace.

Lesson 3: Day 1

> But thou, O Lord art my protector, my glory,
> and the lifter up of my head.
> Psalm 3:4

Trace and copy the verse below.

But thou, O Lord art

my protector, my glory,

and the lifter up of my head.

But thou, O Lord art

my protector, my glory,

and the lifter up of my head.

Psalms & Proverbs for Young Catholics © 2016 Not to be reproduced.

Lesson 3: Day 2

> I have cried to the Lord with my voice:
> and he hath heard me from his holy hill.
> Psalm 3:5

Trace and copy the verse below.

I have cried to the Lord with my voice: and he hath heard me from his holy hill.

I have cried to the Lord with my voice: and he hath heard me from his holy hill.

Lesson 3: Day 3

> Be angry, and sin not: the things you say in your hearts,
> be sorry for them upon your beds.
> Psalm 4:5

Trace and copy the verse below.

Lesson 3: Day 4

> The light of thy countenance O Lord, is signed upon us:
> thou hast given gladness in my heart.
> Psalm 4:7

Trace and copy the verse below.

The light of thy countenance

O Lord, is signed upon us: thou

hast given gladness in my heart.

countenance: face

The light of thy countenance

O Lord, is signed upon us: thou

hast given gladness in my heart.

Lesson 4: Day 1

> Take hold on instruction, leave it not:
> keep it, because it is thy life.
> Proverbs 4:13

Trace and copy the verse below.

Take hold on instruction,

leave it not: keep it,

because it is thy life.

Take hold on instruction,

leave it not: keep it,

because it is thy life.

Lesson 4: Day 2

> Be not delighted in the paths of the wicked,
> neither let the way of evil men please thee.
> Proverbs 4:14

Trace and copy the verse below.

Be not delighted in the paths

of the wicked, neither let the way

of evil men please thee.

Be not delighted in the paths

of the wicked, neither let the way

of evil men please thee.

Lesson 4: Day 3

> Go to the ant, O sluggard,
> and consider her ways, and learn wisdom:
> Proverbs 6:6

Trace and copy the verse below.

Go to the ant, O sluggard,

and consider her ways,

and learn wisdom:

> sluggard: lazy person

Go to the ant, O sluggard,

and consider her ways,

and learn wisdom:

Lesson 4: Day 4

> Keep my commandments, and thou shalt live:
> and my law as the apple of thy eye:
> Proverbs 7:2

Trace and copy the verse below.

Keep my commandments, and

thou shalt live: and my law

as the apple of thy eye:

Keep my commandments, and

thou shalt live: and my law

as the apple of thy eye:

Lesson 5: Day 1

> Hearken to the voice of my prayer,
> O my King and my God.
> Psalm 5:3

Trace and copy the verse below.

Hearken to the voice of

my prayer, O my King

and my God.

> hearken: listen

Hearken to the voice of

my prayer, O my King

and my God.

Psalms & Proverbs for Young Catholics © 2016 Not to be reproduced.

Lesson 5: Day 2

> For to thee will I pray:
> O Lord, in the morning thou shalt hear my voice.
> Psalm 5:4

Trace and copy the verse below.

For to thee will I pray:

O Lord, in the morning

thou shalt hear my voice.

For to thee will I pray:

O Lord, in the morning

thou shalt hear my voice.

Lesson 5: Day 3

> Turn to me, O Lord, and deliver my soul:
> O save me for thy mercy's sake.
> Psalm 6:5

Trace and copy the verse below.

Turn to me, O Lord, and deliver my soul: O save me for thy mercy's sake.

Turn to me, O Lord, and deliver my soul: O save me for thy mercy's sake.

Lesson 5: Day 4

> The Lord hath heard my supplication:
> the Lord hath received my prayer.
> Psalm 6:10

Trace and copy the verse below.

The Lord hath heard my

supplication: the Lord

hath received my prayer.

supplication: an earnest request

The Lord hath heard my

supplication: the Lord

hath received my prayer.

Lesson 6: Day 1

> For wisdom is better than all the most precious things:
> Proverbs 8:11a

Trace and copy the verse below.

For wisdom is

better than all

the most precious things:

For wisdom is

better than all

the most precious things:

Lesson 6: Day 2

> and whatsoever may be desired cannot be compared to it.
> Proverbs 8:11b

Trace and copy the verse below.

and whatsoever may

be desired cannot

be compared to it.

and whatsoever may

be desired cannot

be compared to it.

Lesson 6: Day 3

> Rebuke not a scorner lest he hate thee.
> Rebuke a wise man, and he will love thee.
> Proverbs 9:8

Trace and copy the verse below.

Rebuke not a scorner lest he hate thee. Rebuke a wise man, and he will love thee.

| rebuke: to express disapproval | scorner: one who treats things with contempt |

Rebuke not a scorner lest he hate thee. Rebuke a wise man, and he will love thee.

Psalms & Proverbs for Young Catholics © 2016 Not to be reproduced.

Lesson 6: Day 4

> The fear of the Lord is the beginning of wisdom:
> and the knowledge of the holy is prudence.
> Proverbs 9:10

Trace and copy the verse below.

The fear of the Lord is the beginning

of wisdom: and the knowledge

of the holy is prudence.

prudence: cautiousness

The fear of the Lord is the beginning

of wisdom: and the knowledge

of the holy is prudence.

Lesson 7: Day 1

> O Lord my God, in thee have I put my trust:
> Psalm 7:2a

Trace and copy the verse below.

O Lord my God,

in thee have

I put my trust.

O Lord my God,

in thee have

I put my trust.

Lesson 7: Day 2

> save me from all them that persecute me, and deliver me.
> Psalm 7:2b

Trace and copy the verse below.

save me from all them

that persecute me,

and deliver me.

persecute: to treat badly

save me from all them

that persecute me,

and deliver me.

Lesson 7: Day 3

> O Lord our Lord,
> how admirable is thy name in the whole earth!
> Psalm 8:2a

Trace and copy the verse below.

O Lord our Lord,

how admirable is thy name

in the whole earth!

---

admirable: deserving of respect

O Lord our Lord,

how admirable is thy name

in the whole earth!

Lesson 7: Day 4

> For thy magnificence
> is elevated above the heavens.
> Psalm 8:2b

Trace and copy the verse below.

For thy magnificence

is elevated

above the heavens.

elevated: raised

For thy magnificence

is elevated

above the heavens.

Lesson 8: Day 1

> A wise son maketh the father glad:
> but a foolish son is the sorrow of his mother.
> Proverbs 10:1

Trace and copy the verse below.

A wise son maketh the father

glad: but a foolish son

is the sorrow of his mother.

A wise son maketh the father

glad: but a foolish son

is the sorrow of his mother.

Lesson 8: Day 2

> Hatred stirreth up strifes:
> and charity covereth all sins.
> Proverbs 10:12

Trace and copy the verse below.

Hatred stirreth up strifes:

and charity

covereth all sins.

Hatred stirreth up strifes:

and charity

covereth all sins.

Lesson 8: Day 3

> He that trusteth in his riches shall fall:
> but the just shall spring up as a green leaf.
> Proverbs 11:28

Trace and copy the verse below.

He that trusteth in his riches

shall fall: but the just

shall spring up as a green leaf.

He that trusteth in his riches

shall fall: but the just

shall spring up as a green leaf.

Lesson 8: Day 4

> The fruit of the just man is a tree of life:
> and he that gaineth souls, is wise.
> Proverbs 11:30

Trace and copy the verse below.

The fruit of the just man

is a tree of life: and he

that gaineth souls, is wise.

The fruit of the just man

is a tree of life: and he

that gaineth souls, is wise.

Lesson 9: Day 1

> I will give praise to thee, O Lord, with my whole heart:
> I will relate all thy wonders.
> Psalm 9:2

Trace and copy the verse below.

I will give praise to thee, O Lord,

with my whole heart:

I will relate all thy wonders.

wonders: miracles

I will give praise to thee, O Lord,

with my whole heart:

I will relate all thy wonders.

Lesson 9: Day 2

> I will be glad and rejoice in thee:
> I will sing to thy name, O thou most high.
> Psalm 9:3

Trace and copy the verse below.

Lesson 9: Day 3

> The Lord is in his holy temple,
> the Lord's throne is in heaven.
> Psalm 10:5a

Trace and copy the verse below.

The Lord is in his holy temple,

the Lord's throne

is in heaven.

The Lord is in his holy temple,

the Lord's throne

is in heaven.

Lesson 9: Day 4

> For the Lord is just, and hath loved justice:
> his countenance hath beheld righteousness.
> Psalm 10:8

Trace and copy the verse below.

For the Lord is just, and hath loved justice: his countenance hath beheld righteousness.

For the Lord is just, and hath loved justice: his countenance hath beheld righteousness.

Lesson 10: Day 1

> He that loveth correction, loveth knowledge:
> but he that hateth reproof is foolish.
> Proverbs 12:1

Trace and copy the verse below.

He that loveth correction, loveth

knowledge: but he that

hateth reproof is foolish.

> reproof: an expression of blame

He that loveth correction, loveth

knowledge: but he that

hateth reproof is foolish.

Lesson 10: Day 2

> Lying lips are an abomination to the Lord:
> but they that deal faithfully please him.
> Proverbs 12:22

Trace and copy the verse below.

Lying lips are an abomination

to the Lord: but they that

deal faithfully please him.

> abomination: a thing that causes disgust or hatred

Lying lips are an abomination

to the Lord: but they that

deal faithfully please him.

Lesson 10: Day 3

> Hope that is deferred afflicteth the soul:
> desire when it cometh is a tree of life.
> Proverbs 13:12

Trace and copy the verse below.

Hope that is deferred afflicteth

the soul: desire when it cometh

is a tree of life.

> deferred: to put off to a later time

Hope that is deferred afflicteth

the soul: desire when it cometh

is a tree of life.

Lesson 10: Day 4

> He that walketh with the wise, shall be wise:
> a friend of fools shall become like to them.
> Proverbs 13:20

Trace and copy the verse below.

He that walketh with the wise,

shall be wise: a friend of fools

shall become like to them.

He that walketh with the wise,

shall be wise: a friend of fools

shall become like to them.

Bible History

The word "Bible" comes from the Greek work *biblia*, which means "books." The Bible is a collection of many books. It took many many years--about 1100--to gather them all together in what we now call the Bible.

When the books were written, they did not have computers, or typewriters, or even paper as we do today. They had *papyrus*, a paper-like material made out of reeds, or dried animal skin called *vellum*. Can you imagine writing on such things? We are so accustomed to having lots of paper, it is hard for us to think about writing a book report or a whole book using only these materials.

Bible History

Oh, and they didn't have pens or pencils like we do. They had quills pens which were made from the feathers of birds. It probably sounds like a lot of fun but if you had to do it all the time for all your writing, you might get tired of it.

Try finding a large feather, cutting the end off of the shaft, dipping it in ink and try writing like the scribes of old!

Lesson 11: Day 1

> But I have trusted in thy mercy.
> My heart shall rejoice in thy salvation:
> Psalm 12:6a

Trace and copy the verse below.

But I have trusted

in thy mercy. My heart

shall rejoice in thy salvation:

But I have trusted

in thy mercy. My heart

shall rejoice in thy salvation:

Lesson 11: Day 2

> I will sing to the Lord, who giveth me good things:
> yea I will sing to the name of the Lord the most high.
> Psalm 12:6b

Trace and copy the verse below.

Lesson 11: Day 3

> The Lord hath looked down from heaven
> upon the children of men,
> Psalm 13:2a

Trace and copy the verse below.

The Lord hath looked down

from heaven upon

the children of men,

The Lord hath looked down

from heaven upon

the children of men,

Lesson 11: Day 4

> to see if there be any
> that understand and seek God.
> Psalm 13:2b

Trace and copy the verse below.

to see if there be any

that understand

and seek God.

to see if there be any

that understand

and seek God.

Lesson 12: Day 1

> A faithful witness will not lie:
> but a deceitful witness uttereth a lie.
> Proverbs 14:5

Trace and copy the verse below.

A faithful witness will not lie:

but a deceitful witness

uttereth a lie.

> deceitful: misleading

A faithful witness will not lie:

but a deceitful witness

uttereth a lie.

Lesson 12: Day 2

> There is a way which seemeth just to a man:
> but the ends thereof lead to death.
> Proverbs 14:12

Trace and copy the verse below.

There is a way which seemeth just to a man: but the ends thereof lead to death.

There is a way which seemeth just to a man: but the ends thereof lead to death.

Lesson 12: Day 3

> A mild answer breaketh wrath:
> but a harsh word stirreth up fury.
> Proverbs 15:1

Trace and copy the verse below.

A mild answer breaketh wrath:

but a harsh word

stirreth up fury.

| wrath: extreme anger | harsh: cruel |

A mild answer breaketh wrath:

but a harsh word

stirreth up fury.

Lesson 12: Day 4

> Better is a little with the fear of the Lord,
> than great treasures without content,
> Proverbs 15:16

Trace and copy the verse below.

Better is a little with the fear

of the Lord, than great treasures

without content,

Better is a little with the fear

of the Lord, than great treasures

without content,

Lesson 13: Day 1

> I set the Lord always in my sight:
> for he is at my right hand, that I be not moved.
> Psalm 15:8

Trace and copy the verse below.

Lesson 13: Day 2

> Thou hast made known to me the ways of life,
> thou shalt fill me with joy with thy countenance:
> at thy right hand are delights even to the end.
> Proverbs 15:11

Trace and copy the verse below.

Thou hast made known to me

the ways of life,

thou shalt fill me with joy

with thy countenance:

at thy right hand

are delights even to the end.

Lesson 13: Day 3

Praising I will call upon the Lord:
and I shall be saved from my enemies.
Psalm 17:4

Trace and copy the verse below.

Praising I will call upon
the Lord: and I shall be saved
from my enemies.

Praising I will call upon
the Lord: and I shall be saved
from my enemies.

Lesson 13: Day 4

> For thou lightest my lamp, O Lord:
> O my God enlighten my darkness.
> Psalm 17:29

Trace and copy the verse below.

Lesson 14: Day 1

> Better is a little with justice,
> than great revenues with iniquity.
> Proverbs 16:8

Trace and copy the verse below.

Better is a little with justice,

than great revenues

with iniquity.

| revenues: income | iniquity: immoral, unfair behavior |

Better is a little with justice,

than great revenues

with iniquity.

Lesson 14: Day 2

> Pride goeth before destruction:
> and the spirit is lifted up before a fall.
> Proverbs 16:18

Trace and copy the verse below.

Pride goeth before destruction:

and the spirit

is lifted up before a fall.

Pride goeth before destruction:

and the spirit

is lifted up before a fall.

Lesson 14: Day 3

> As silver is tried by fire, and gold in the furnace:
> so the Lord trieth the hearts.
> Proverbs 17:3

Trace and copy the verse below.

As silver is tried by fire,

and gold in the furnace:

so the Lord trieth the hearts.

As silver is tried by fire,

and gold in the furnace:

so the Lord trieth the hearts.

Lesson 14 : Day 4

> He that is a friend loveth at all times:
> and a brother is proved in distress.
> Proverbs 17:17

Trace and copy the verse below.

He that is a friend

loveth at all times: and a

brother is proved in distress.

distress: suffering

He that is a friend

loveth at all times: and a

brother is proved in distress.

Lesson 15: Day 1

> The heavens shew forth the glory of God,
> and the firmament declareth the work of his hands.
> Psalm 18:2

Trace and copy the verse below.

The heavens shew forth the glory of God, and the firmament declareth the work of his hands.

firmament: the heavens, sky

The heavens shew forth the glory of God, and the firmament declareth the work of his hands.

Lesson 15 : Day 2

> And the words of my mouth shall be such as may please:
> and the meditation of my heart always in thy sight.
> O Lord, my helper, and my redeemer.
> Psalm 18:15

Trace and copy the verse below.

And the words of my mouth

shall be such as may please:

and the meditation of my heart

meditation: thoughts

always in thy sight.

O Lord, my helper,

and my redeemer.

Lesson 15: Day 3

> May the Lord hear thee in the day of tribulation:
> may the name of the God of Jacob protect thee.
> Psalm 19:2

Trace and copy the verse below.

May the Lord hear thee in the day of tribulation: may the name of the God of Jacob protect thee.

tribulation: great trouble

May the Lord hear thee in the day of tribulation: may the name of the God of Jacob protect thee.

Lesson 15: Day 4

> Some trust in chariots, and some in horses:
> but we will call upon the name of the Lord our God.
> Psalm 19:8

Trace and copy the verse below.

Some trust in chariots, and some

in horses: but we will call upon

the name of the Lord our God.

Some trust in chariots, and some

in horses: but we will call upon

the name of the Lord our God.

Lesson 16: Day 1

> The learning of a man is known by patience
> and his glory is to pass over wrongs.
> Proverbs 19:11

Trace and copy the verse below.

The learning of a man is known

by patience and his glory

is to pass over wrongs.

The learning of a man is known

by patience and his glory

is to pass over wrongs.

Psalms & Proverbs for Young Catholics © 2016 Not to be reproduced.

Lesson 16: Day 2

> He that hath mercy on the poor, lendeth to the Lord:
> and he will repay him.
> Proverbs 19:17

Trace and copy the verse below.

He that hath mercy on the poor,

lendeth to the Lord:

and he will repay him.

He that hath mercy on the poor,

lendeth to the Lord:

and he will repay him.

Lesson 16: Day 3

> Hear counsel, and receive instruction,
> that thou mayst be wise in thy latter end.
> Proverbs 19:20

Trace and copy the verse below.

Hear counsel, and receive instruction, that thou mayst be wise in thy latter end.

Hear counsel, and receive instruction, that thou mayst be wise in thy latter end.

Lesson 16: Day 4

> There are many thoughts in the heart of a man:
> but the will of the Lord shall stand firm.
> Proverbs 19:21

Trace and copy the verse below.

Lesson 17: Day 1

> Be thou exalted, O Lord, in thy own strength:
> we will sing and praise thy power.
> Psalm 20:14

Trace and copy the verse below.

Be thou exalted, O Lord,

in thy own strength: we will

sing and praise thy power.

Be thou exalted, O Lord,

in thy own strength: we will

sing and praise thy power.

Lesson 17: Day 2

> For the kingdom is the Lord's;
> and he shall have dominion over the nations.
> Psalm 21:29

Trace and copy the verse below.

For the kingdom is the Lord's;

and he shall have

dominion over the nations.

dominion: control

For the kingdom is the Lord's;

and he shall have

dominion over the nations.

Lesson 17: Day 3

> For though I should walk in the midst of the shadow of death,
> I will fear no evils,
> Psalm 22:4a

Trace and copy the verse below.

For though I should walk in

the midst of the shadow

of death, I will fear no evils,

For though I should walk in

the midst of the shadow

of death, I will fear no evils,

Lesson 17: Day 4

> for thou art with me.
> Thy rod and thy staff, they have comforted me.
> Psalm 22:4b

Trace and copy the verse below.

for thou art with me.

Thy rod and thy staff,

they have comforted me.

for thou art with me.

Thy rod and thy staff,

they have comforted me.

Lesson 18: Day 1

> Every way of a man seemeth right to himself:
> but the Lord weigheth the hearts.
> Proverbs 21:2

Trace and copy the verse below.

Every way of a man seemeth

right to himself: but the Lord

weigheth the hearts.

weigheth: tests, examines

Every way of a man seemeth

right to himself: but the Lord

weigheth the hearts.

Lesson 18: Day 2

> He that followeth justice and mercy,
> shall find life, justice, and glory.
> Proverbs 21:21

Trace and copy the verse below.

He that followeth justice

and mercy, shall find

life, justice, and glory.

He that followeth justice

and mercy, shall find

life, justice, and glory.

Lesson 18: Day 3

> A good name is better than great riches:
> and good favour is above silver and gold.
> Proverbs 22:1

Trace and copy the verse below.

A good name is better than great riches: and good favour is above silver and gold.

A good name is better than great riches: and good favour is above silver and gold.

Lesson 18: Day 4

> The rich ruleth over the poor:
> and the borrower is servant to him that lendeth.
> Proverbs 22:7

Trace and copy the verse below.

The rich ruleth over the poor:

and the borrower is servant

to him that lendeth.

The rich ruleth over the poor:

and the borrower is servant

to him that lendeth.

Lesson 19: Day 1

> Who is this King of Glory?
> the Lord of hosts, he is the King of Glory.
> Psalm 23:10

Trace and copy the verse below.

Who is this King of Glory?

the Lord of hosts,

he is the King of Glory.

Who is this King of Glory?

the Lord of hosts,

he is the King of Glory.

Lesson 19: Day 2

> In thee, O my God, I put my trust;
> let me not be ashamed.
> Psalm 24:2

Trace and copy the verse below.

In thee, O my God,

I put my trust;

let me not be ashamed.

In thee, O my God,

I put my trust;

let me not be ashamed.

Lesson 19: Day 3

> I have loved, O Lord, the beauty of thy house;
> and the place where thy glory dwelleth.
> Psalm 25:8

Trace and copy the verse below.

I have loved, O Lord, the beauty of thy house; and the place where thy glory dwelleth.

dwelleth: lives

I have loved, O Lord, the beauty of thy house; and the place where thy glory dwelleth.

Lesson 19: Day 4

> One thing I have asked of the Lord, this will I seek after;
> that I may dwell in the house of the Lord all the days of my life.
> That I may see the delight of the Lord, and may visit his temple.
> Psalm 26:4

Trace and copy the verse below.

One thing I have asked of

the Lord, this will I seek after;

that I may dwell in the house

delight: pleasure

of the Lord all the days of my life.

That I may see the delight of the

Lord, and may visit his temple.

Lesson 20: Day 1

> My son, if thy mind be wise,
> my heart shall rejoice with thee:
> Proverbs 23:15

Trace and copy the verse below.

My son, if thy mind

be wise, my heart

shall rejoice with thee:

My son, if thy mind

be wise, my heart

shall rejoice with thee:

Lesson 20: Day 2

> Let not thy heart envy sinners:
> but be thou in the fear of the Lord all the day long:
> Proverbs 23:17

Trace and copy the verse below.

Lesson 20: Day 3

> By wisdom the house shall be built,
> and by prudence it shall be strengthened.
> Proverbs 24:3

Trace and copy the verse below.

By wisdom the house shall

be built, and by prudence

it shall be strengthened.

By wisdom the house shall

be built, and by prudence

it shall be strengthened.

Lesson 20: Day 4

> By instruction the storerooms shall be filled
> with all precious and most beautiful wealth.
> Proverbs 24:4

Trace and copy the verse below.

By instruction the storerooms

shall be filled with all precious

and most beautiful wealth.

By instruction the storerooms

shall be filled with all precious

and most beautiful wealth.

Translating the Scriptures

Timeline of Bible Translation

(A.D. stands for *anno Domini*--"in the year of the Lord")

- 180 A.D. The New Testament starts to be translated from Greek into Latin, Syriac, and Coptic.

- 195 A.D. The name of the first translation of the Old and New Testaments into Latin was termed Old Latin, both Testaments having been translated from the Greek. Parts of the Old Latin were found in quotes by the church father Tertullian, who lived around 160-220 A.D. in north Africa and wrote treatises on theology.

- 300 A.D. The Old Syriac was a translation of the New Testament from the Greek into Syriac.

- 300 A.D. The Coptic Versions: Coptic was spoken in four dialects in Egypt. The Bible was translated into each of these four dialects.

- 380 A.D. The Latin Vulgate was translated by St. Jerome. He translated into Latin the Old Testament from the Hebrew and the New Testament from Greek. The Latin Vulgate became the Bible of the Western Church until the Protestant Reformation in the 1500's. It continues to be the authoritative translation of the Roman Catholic Church to this day.

- 1380 A.D. The first English translation of the Bible was by John Wycliffe. He translated the Bible into English from the Latin Vulgate. This was a translation from a translation and not a translation from the original Hebrew and Greek. Wycliffe was forced to translate from the Latin Vulgate because he did not know Hebrew or Greek.

- 1440s A.D. Gutenberg invents the printing press and publishes the Gutenberg Bible in the Latin Vulgate.

- 1500s A.D. The Protestant Reformation saw an increase in translations of the Bible into the common languages of the people.

- 1611 A.D. The King James Bible, translated from Greek, Hebrew, and Aramaic, is completed by 47 scholars for the Church of England, and replaced the Wycliffe Bible as the official English translation of the Bible.

Bible translation continues today! In the last fifty years, Bible scholars and translators have released many new English versions of the Bible, including the New King James Version, the English Standard Version, the New American Standard Bible, the New International Version, the New Living Translation, and many more. The Bible has also been translated into many languages around the world. According to Wycliffe Bible Translators, as of 2015:

- More than 1,300 languages have access to the New Testament and some portions of Scripture in their language.
- More than 550 languages have the complete translated Bible.
- About 7,000 languages are known to be in use today.
- Up to 180 million people need Bible translation to begin in their language.
- Just under 2,300 languages across 130 countries have active translation and linguistic development work happening right now.
- Up to 1,800 languages still need a Bible translation project to begin.

Copying the Scriptures

Most people in our country can read and many own several Bibles. But for a long time, it was very expensive to purchase a Bible. Also, very few people knew how to read. Therefore, few people owned a Bible. Can you imagine not being able to read your favorite book? That would be simply terrible. Some would say we are lucky, but really we are very blessed. If you ever feel like grumbling about your reading time, think about how many books you have. It might help you to have a change in your attitude.

In about 1456, a man named Johannes Gutenburg, invented the printing press. Wonder of wonders, something that used to take years to print by hand, letter by letter, could now be done very quickly on his printing press. That is when books started to become more available and less expensive. We can thank Mr. Gutenburg for making it possible for us to have all the books we want: easy books, hard books, books about math and science, and even books about your favorite games.

You can see very old copies of the Old and New Testaments in museums all around the world. This might be a fun field trip for you and your family to take.

Lesson 21: Day 1

> Blessed be the Lord,
> for he hath heard the voice of my supplication.
> Psalm 27:6

Trace and copy the verse below.

Blessed be the Lord,

for he hath heard

the voice of my supplication.

Blessed be the Lord,

for he hath heard

the voice of my supplication.

Lesson 21: Day 2

> Bring to the Lord glory and honour:
> bring to the Lord glory to his name:
> Psalm 28:2a

Trace and copy the verse below.

Bring the Lord glory

and honour: bring to

the Lord glory to his name:

Bring the Lord glory

and honour: bring to

the Lord glory to his name:

Lesson 21: Day 3

> Sing to the Lord, O ye his saints:
> and give praise to the memory of his holiness.
> Psalm 29:5

Trace and copy the verse below.

Sing to the Lord, O ye his saints:

and give praise

to the memory of his holiness.

Sing to the Lord, O ye his saints:

and give praise

to the memory of his holiness.

Lesson 21: Day 4

> Make thy face to shine upon thy servant;
> save me in thy mercy.
> Psalm 30:17

Trace and copy the verse below.

Lesson 22: Day 1

> It is the glory of God to conceal the word,
> and the glory of kings to search out the speech.
> Proverbs 25:2

Trace and copy the verse below.

Psalms & Proverbs for Young Catholics © 2016 Not to be reproduced.

Lesson 22: Day 2

> To speak a word in due time,
> is like apples of gold on beds of silver.
> Proverbs 25:11

Trace and copy the verse below.

To speak a word in due time,

is like apples of gold

on beds of silver.

To speak a word in due time,

is like apples of gold

on beds of silver.

Lesson 22: Day 3

> If thy enemy be hungry, give him to eat:
> if he thirst, give him water to drink:
> Proverbs 25:21

Trace and copy the verse below.

If thy enemy be hungry,

give him to eat: if he thirst,

give him water to drink:

If thy enemy be hungry,

give him to eat: if he thirst,

give him water to drink:

Psalms & Proverbs for Young Catholics © 2016 Not to be reproduced.

Lesson 22: Day 4

> For thou shalt heap hot coals upon his head,
> and the Lord will reward thee.
> Proverbs 25:22

Trace and copy the verse below.

For thou shalt heap

hot coals upon his head,

and the Lord will reward thee.

For thou shalt heap

hot coals upon his head,

and the Lord will reward thee.

Lesson 23: Day 1

> Blessed are they whose iniquities are forgiven,
> and whose sins are covered.
> Psalm 31:1

Trace and copy the verse below.

Blessed are they whose

iniquities are forgiven,

and whose sins are covered.

Blessed are they whose

iniquities are forgiven,

and whose sins are covered.

Lesson 23: Day 2

> Be glad in the Lord, and rejoice, ye just,
> and glory, all ye right of heart.
> Psalm 31:11

Trace and copy the verse below.

Lesson 23: Day 3

> For the word of the Lord is right,
> and all his works are done with faithfulness.
> Psalm 32:4

Trace and copy the verse below.

For the word of the Lord is right,

and all his works

are done with faithfulness.

For the word of the Lord is right,

and all his works

are done with faithfulness.

Lesson 23: Day 4

> Blessed is the nation whose God is the Lord:
> the people whom he hath chosen for his inheritance.
> Psalm 32:12

Trace and copy the verse below.

Blessed is the nation whose God

is the Lord: the people whom he

hath chosen for his inheritance.

> inheritance: rightful possession

Blessed is the nation whose God

is the Lord: the people whom he

hath chosen for his inheritance.

Lesson 24: Day 1

> Let another praise thee, and not thy own mouth:
> a stranger, and not thy own lips.
> Proverbs 27:2

Trace and copy the verse below.

Let another praise thee,

and not thy own mouth:

a stranger, and not thy own lips.

Let another praise thee,

and not thy own mouth:

a stranger, and not thy own lips.

Lesson 24: Day 2

> Better are the wounds of a friend,
> than the deceitful kisses of an enemy.
> Proverbs 27:6

Trace and copy the verse below.

Better are the wounds

of a friend, than the

deceitful kisses of an enemy.

Better are the wounds

of a friend, than the

deceitful kisses of an enemy.

Lesson 24: Day 3

> Iron sharpeneth iron,
> so a man sharpeneth the countenance of his friend.
> Proverbs 27:17

Trace and copy the verse below.

Iron sharpeneth iron,

so a man sharpeneth

the countenance of his friend.

Iron sharpeneth iron,

so a man sharpeneth

the countenance of his friend.

Lesson 24: Day 4

> Better is the poor man walking in his simplicity,
> than the rich in crooked ways.
> Proverbs 28:6

Trace and copy the verse below.

Better is the poor man

walking in his simplicity,

than the rich in crooked ways.

Better is the poor man

walking in his simplicity,

than the rich in crooked ways.

Lesson 25: Day 1

> I will bless the Lord at all times,
> his praise shall be always in my mouth.
> Psalms 33:2

Trace and copy the verse below.

Lesson 25: Day 2

> I sought the Lord, and he heard me;
> and he delivered me from all my troubles.
> Psalm 33:5

Trace and copy the verse below.

I sought the Lord, and he

heard me; and he delivered me

from all my troubles.

I sought the Lord, and he

heard me; and he delivered me

from all my troubles.

Lesson 25: Day 3

> O taste, and see that the Lord is sweet:
> blessed is the man that hopeth in him.
> Psalm 33:9

Trace and copy the verse below.

Lesson 25: Day 4

> Turn away from evil and do good:
> seek after peace and pursue it.
> Psalm 33:15

Trace and copy the verse below.

Lesson 26: Day 1

> In the joy of the just there is great glory:
> when the wicked reign, men are ruined.
> Proverbs 28:12

Trace and copy the verse below.

In the joy of the just there is great glory: when the wicked reign, men are ruined.

reign: rule

In the joy of the just there is great glory: when the wicked reign, men are ruined.

Lesson 26: Day 2

> He that walketh uprightly, shall be saved:
> he that is perverse in his ways shall fall at once.
> Proverbs 28:18

Trace and copy the verse below.

He that walketh uprightly,

shall be saved: he that is perverse

in his ways shall fall at once.

> perverse: unacceptable, wrong

He that walketh uprightly,

shall be saved: he that is perverse

in his ways shall fall at once.

Lesson 26: Day 3

> A faithful man shall be much praised:
> but he that maketh haste to be rich, shall not be innocent.
> Proverbs 28:20

Trace and copy the verse below.

Lesson 26: Day 4

> The king that judgeth the poor in truth,
> his throne shall be established for ever.
> Proverbs 29:14

Trace and copy the verse below.

The king that judgeth the poor

in truth, his throne

shall be established for ever.

The king that judgeth the poor

in truth, his throne

shall be established for ever.

# Lesson 27: Day 1

> I will give thanks to thee in a great church;
> I will praise thee in a strong people.
> Psalm 34:18

Trace and copy the verse below.

I will give thanks to thee in a great church; I will praise thee in a strong people.

I will give thanks to thee in a great church; I will praise thee in a strong people.

Lesson 27: Day 2

> Thou hast seen, O Lord, be not thou silent:
> O Lord, depart not from me.
> Psalm 34:22

Trace and copy the verse below.

Thou hast seen, O Lord,

be not thou silent:

O Lord, depart not from me.

Thou hast seen, O Lord,

be not thou silent:

O Lord, depart not from me.

Lesson 27: Day 3

> And my tongue shall meditate thy justice,
> thy praise all the day long.
> Psalm 34:28

Trace and copy the verse below.

And my tongue shall

meditate thy justice,

thy praise all the day long.

And my tongue shall

meditate thy justice,

thy praise all the day long.

Lesson 27: Day 4

> For with thee is the fountain of life;
> and in thy light we shall see light.
> Psalm 35:10

Trace and copy the verse below.

Lesson 28: Day 1

> Corrupt men bring a city to ruin:
> but wise men turn away wrath.
> Proverbs 29:8

Trace and copy the verse below.

Corrupt men bring a city

to ruin: but wise men

turn away wrath.

corrupt: dishonest, evil

Corrupt men bring a city

to ruin: but wise men

turn away wrath.

Lesson 28: Day 2

> Instruct thy son, and he shall refresh thee,
> and shall give delight to thy soul.
> Proverbs 29:17

Trace and copy the verse below.

Instruct thy son, and he shall refresh thee, and shall give delight to thy soul.

Instruct thy son, and he shall refresh thee, and shall give delight to thy soul.

Lesson 28: Day 3

> Humiliation followeth the proud:
> and glory shall uphold the humble of spirit.
> Proverbs 29:23

Trace and copy the verse below.

Humiliation followeth the proud:

and glory shall uphold

the humble of spirit.

humiliation: being shamed

Humiliation followeth the proud:

and glory shall uphold

the humble of spirit.

Lesson 28: Day 4

> He that feareth man, shall quickly fall:
> he that trusteth in the Lord, shall be set on high.
> Proverbs 29:25

Trace and copy the verse below.

He that feareth man, shall quickly

fall: he that trusteth in the Lord,

shall be set on high.

He that feareth man, shall quickly

fall: he that trusteth in the Lord,

shall be set on high.

Lesson 29: Day 1

> Trust in the Lord, and do good, and dwell in the land,
> and thou shalt be fed with its riches.
> Psalm 36:3

Trace and copy the verse below.

Trust in the Lord, and do good,

and dwell in the land, and thou

shalt be fed with its riches.

Trust in the Lord, and do good,

and dwell in the land, and thou

shalt be fed with its riches.

Lesson 29: Day 2

> Delight in the Lord,
> and he will give thee the requests of thy heart.
> Psalm 36:4

Trace and copy the verse below.

Delight in the Lord,

and he will give thee

the requests of thy heart.

> requests: things asked for

Delight in the Lord,

and he will give thee

the requests of thy heart.

Lesson 29: Day 3

> Commit thy way to the Lord,
> and trust in him, and he will do it.
> Psalm 36:5

Trace and copy the verse below.

Commit thy way to the Lord,

and trust in him,

and he will do it.

Commit thy way to the Lord,

and trust in him,

and he will do it.

Lesson 29: Day 4

> With the Lord shall the steps
> of a man be directed,
> Psalm 36:23a

Trace and copy the verse below.

With the Lord

shall the steps

of a man be directed,

With the Lord

shall the steps

of a man be directed,

Lesson 30: Day 1

> Every word of God is fire tried:
> he is a buckler to them that hope in him.
> Proverbs 30:5

Trace and copy the verse below.

Every word of God is

fire tried: he is a buckler

to them that hope in him.

| fire tried: tested by fire, pure | buckler: a small, round shield |

Every word of God is

fire tried: he is a buckler

to them that hope in him.

Lesson 30: Day 2

> Add not any thing to his words,
> lest thou be reproved, and found a liar:
> Proverbs 30:6

Trace and copy the verse below.

Add not any thing to his words,

lest thou be reproved,

and found a liar:

Add not any thing to his words,

lest thou be reproved,

and found a liar:

Lesson 30: Day 3

> Open thy mouth, decree that which is just,
> and do justice to the needy and poor.
> Proverbs 31:9

Trace and copy the verse below.

Open thy mouth, decree that which is just, and do justice to the needy and poor.

decree: to make an official order or law

Open thy mouth, decree that which is just, and do justice to the needy and poor.

Lesson 30: Day 4

> Favour is deceitful, and beauty is vain:
> the woman that feareth the Lord, she shall be praised.
> Proverbs 31:30

Trace and copy the verse below.

Items available from Laurelwood Books:

Ōlim, Once Upon a Time, in Latin Series:
Book I (reader and workbook): The Three Little Pigs, The Tortoise and the Hare,
The Crow and the Pitcher
Book II (reader and workbook): The Ant and the Chrysalis, The Lost Sheep,
The Good Samaritan
Book III (reader and workbook) - The Feeding of the 5,000, The Lion and the Mouse
Book IV (reader and workbook) - Creation
Book V (reader and workbook) - Daniel, Part I; We Know a Tree by its Fruit
Book VI (reader and workbook) - The Prodigal Son
book VII (reader and workbook) - David and Goliath
Book VIII (reader and workbook) - Daniel, Part II
Book IX (reader and workbook) - Daniel, Part III, The Miser
Book X (reader and workbook) - The Wise Man and Foolish Man, The Ten Maidens

Ōlim Derivatives I
Ōlim Derivatives II
Latin Verbs: To Infinitives and Beyond! Book I

Scripture Scribes Series
Pre-Primary: *From Scribbler to Scribe*
Primary: *Who Made Me?, My Whole Heart, His Name Is Wonderful, Practicing Proverbs, Psalms & Proverbs for Young Catholics*
Intermediate: *One Another, Savoring Psalms*
Upper School: *Men of Honor & Women of Grace, Walking With God*

Patriotic Penmanship Series for Grades K-12
Also Available: Jump Rope Review Book, Transition to Cursive Book,
Dinosaur Review Book

State The Facts: A Guide to Studying Your State Whether you are studying the state you live in or any other state, this book offers your student the opportunity to research and learn state history, geography, weather, and more!

Study Guides:
Based on Rosemary Sutcliff's historical fiction
*The Eagle of the Ninth • The Silver Branch Outcast • The Lantern Bearers
Warrior Scarlet • Sword Song • The Shining Company*

Based on Emma Leslie's historical fiction:
Out of the Mouth of the Lion
Glaucia the Greek Slave

Laurelwood Books offers both new and used curricula to families wishing
to help their children learn and achieve success in school or at home.

To order: www.laurelwoodbooks.com
marylnw7@gmail.com

Made in the USA
Columbia, SC
20 February 2018